TOUCHING THEIR PREY
ANIMALS WITH AN AMAZING SENSE OF TOUCH

written by Kathryn Lay
illustrated by Christina Wald

visit us at www.abdopublishing.com

Printed in the United States of America, North Mankato, Minnesota.
052012
092012
♲ This book contains at least 10% recycled materials.

Written by Kathryn Lay
Illustrated by Christina Wald
Edited by Stephanie Hedlund and Rochelle Baltzer
Cover and interior layout and design by Neil Klinepier

Library of Congress Cataloging-in-Publication Data

Lay, Kathryn.
 Touching their prey : animals with an amazing sense of touch / written by Kathryn Lay ; illustrated by Christina Wald.
     p. cm. -- (Sensing their prey)
 Includes index.
 ISBN 978-1-61641-870-0
 1. Touch--Juvenile literature. 2. Senses and sensation--Juvenile literature. I. Wald, Christina, ill. II. Title.
 QP451.L39 2013
 612.8'8--dc23
                        2011053366

CONTENTS

Dinner by Touch 4

Sensitive Feelers 8

It Might Be Dinner If the Ground Shakes. 11

Paws, Claws, and Whiskers 19

A Hairy Touch. 27

Finding Food on the Floor 28

Feeling Your Food 31

Glossary 32

Index 32

Web Sites 32

DINNER BY TOUCH

Animals must find their own food every day. A predator is an animal that lives by eating other animals. Many predators have strong senses that help them find food. Some animals use their sense of touch to find prey.

You might be told not to play with your food, but that doesn't apply to animals! Some animals smell their prey or see it from far away. Others have special ways to touch and feel to find the food that they like.

What sense would you want to use to find food? Sight, sound, taste, touch, or smell? Why?

Sensitive Feelers

A catfish is not a fish that looks like a cat. But, it does have whiskers called barbels on its face. With these whiskers, a catfish feels its way around in dark water to find food.

It Might Be Dinner If the Ground Shakes

Some animals feel vibrations through parts of their bodies. Snakes are able to feel sound through bones in their lower jaws. This sense of touch helps them find prey.

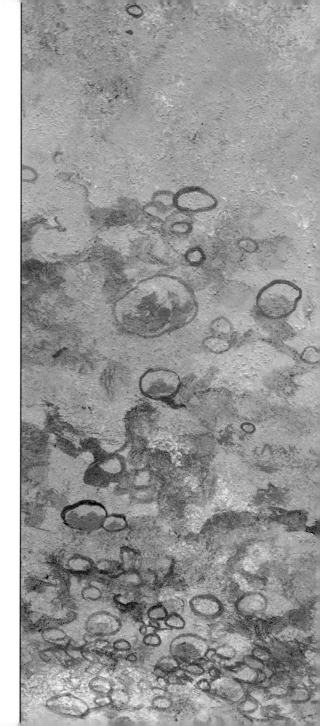

Although a scorpion has bad eyesight, it has an excellent sense of touch. Hairs on its body detect vibrations in the air and on the ground.

A sand scorpion feels vibrations in the sand through its sensory hairs. Then, it can quickly turn and grab the prey with its pincers. Thanks to this strong sense of touch, the scorpion can both find and capture its prey without seeing it first.

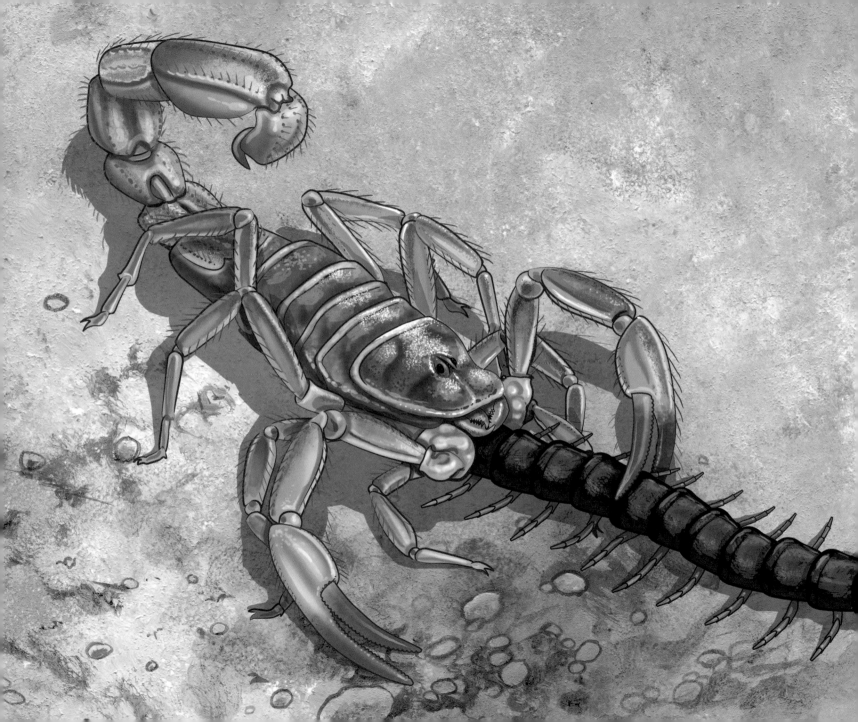

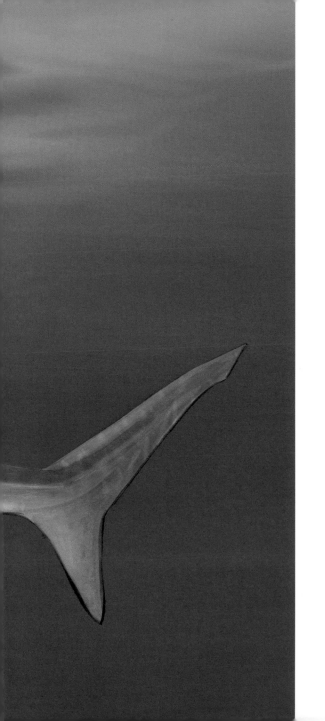

A shark has fluid-filled canals just beneath its skin. These canals are along the sides of its head and body. Underwater noises or motion cause a vibration that strikes pores along the canals. A shark tunes in to the vibration and looks for its next meal.

A tarantula has tiny eyes and poor eyesight. But, it has a good sense of touch. It feels the ground vibrate when its prey is near. It uses the hairs on its body to sense even the slightest vibrations.

You have hairs on your arms. Can you use them to feel the vibrations of the things around you?

Paws, Claws, and Whiskers

Raccoons depend on their sense of touch to hunt. They use their paws to scavenge. They also use them to reach into rivers to fish.

The Gila monster has sensitive claws. Its claws feel the ground to find another animal's burrow. Then, the claws dig out the burrow to find that animal's eggs. These eggs are just what the Gila monster is hoping to eat.

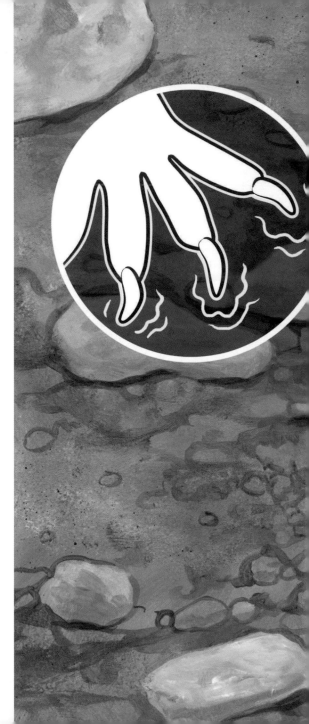

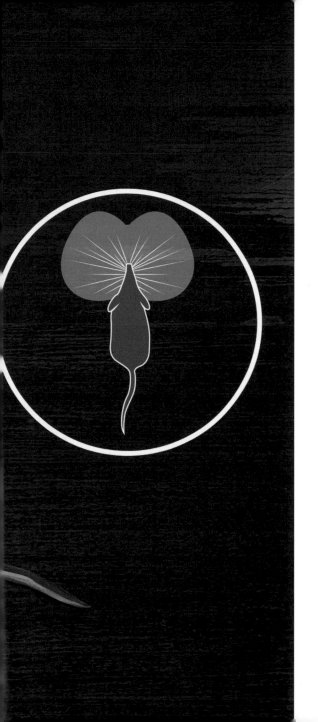

The Etruscan shrew is one of the world's smallest mammals. It is about one and a half inches (4 cm) long and weighs less than one pound (16 oz).

Because it is a nocturnal animal, this shrew uses its sense of touch to hunt at night. The shrew has long whiskers that can find crickets, cockroaches, and spiders. The whiskers tell the shrew's brain what they are touching.

The walrus feels with its whiskers. It pokes its whiskers into the ocean floor until it feels food, such as a crab. Then, the walrus digs out its prey with its tusks.

If you could have one extra special feature to touch things, other than your hands, what would it be? Would you want paws, claws, or whiskers?

A Hairy Touch

Crabs have tiny hairs on their claws and other parts of their body. These hairs help sense water movement and vibration so they can find prey.

FINDING FOOD ON THE FLOOR

Sea otters dive to the bottom of the ocean to find their prey. They have poor eyesight underwater. So, they use their sensitive front paws to feel around for food on the ocean floor.

If you closed your eyes at lunch, you might grab something you didn't like to eat, such as corn on the cob instead of your roll.

FEELING YOUR FOOD

Even with poor sight, smell, or hearing, many predators are able to find food. Their sense of touch helps these animals find prey. Do you feel your stomach rumbling? Maybe you are hungry, too!

GLOSSARY

barbel - a whisker on certain fishes used for sensing touch.

burrow - an underground home for animals.

canal - a passageway.

fluid - a liquid that flows or takes the shape of its container.

nocturnal - active at night.

pincers - claws with jaws that are used for grabbing things.

pore - a small opening that matter passes through.

scavenge - to collect usable things from what others have thrown away.

sensory - related to the senses.

vibrations - tiny back and forth movements.

INDEX

canals 15

catfish 8

claws 20, 27

crab 27

Etruscan shrew 23

Gila monster 20

hairs 12, 16, 27

paws 19, 28

raccoon 19

scorpion 12

sea otter 28

shark 15

snake 11

tarantula 16

vibrations 11, 12, 15, 16, 27

walrus 24

whiskers 8, 23, 24

WEB SITES

To learn more about animal senses, visit ABDO Group online at **www.abdopublishing.com**. Web sites about animal senses are featured on our Book Links page. These links are routinely monitored and updated to provide the most current information available.